The 1940s
Decade in Photos
A World at War

Jim Corrigan

Enslow Publishers, Inc.
40 Industrial Road
Box 398
Berkeley Heights, NJ 07922
USA

http://www.enslow.com

Library of Congress Cataloging-in-Publication Data

Corrigan, Jim.
  The 1940s decade in photos : a world at war / by Jim Corrigan.
      p. cm. — (Amazing decades in photos)
  Includes bibliographical references and index.
  Summary: "Middle school readers will find out about the important world, national, and cultural developments of the decade 1940-1949"—Provided by publisher.
  ISBN-13: 978-0-7660-3133-3
  ISBN-10: 0-7660-3133-0
  1. United States—History—1933–1945—Pictorial works—Juvenile literature. 2. United States—History—1945–1953—Pictorial works—Juvenile literature. 3. History, Modern—20th century—Pictorial works—Juvenile literature. 4. Nineteen forties—Pictorial works—Juvenile literature.
  I. Title. II. Title: Nineteen forties decade in photos.
  E806.C64 2009
  973.917—dc22

                                                                        2008042910

Printed in the United States of America.

092009 Lake Book Manufacturing, Inc., Melrose Park, IL

10 9 8 7 6 5 4 3 2 1

To Our Readers: We have done our best to make sure all Internet Addresses in this book were active and appropriate when we went to press. However, the author and the publisher have no control over and assume no liability for the material available on those Internet sites or on other Web sites they may link to. Any comments or suggestions can be sent by email to comments@enslow.com or to the address on the back cover.

Every effort has been made to locate all copyright holders of material used in this book. If any errors or omissions have occurred, corrections will be made in future editions of this book.

♻ Enslow Publishers, Inc., is committed to printing our books on recycled paper. The paper in every book contains 10% to 30% post-consumer waste (PCW). The cover board on the outside of each book contains 100% PCW. Our goal is to do our part to help young people and the environment too!

Produced by OTTN Publishing, Stockton, N.J.

TABLE OF CONTENTS

An American tank fires a shot while under cover of tree branches. World War II was the most destructive conflict in human history. By the time the war ended in 1945, more than 60 million people had been killed.

WELCOME TO THE *1940s*

*T*he Second World War happened in the 1940s. By far, World War II was the biggest event of the decade. It was the worst conflict in human history. Roughly 60 million people died in the war. The world had never before seen such death and destruction at one time.

At least half of the war's victims were not soldiers. They were civilians. Some of these bystanders were killed in the fighting. Others died of disease and starvation. Many were executed because of their race or religion. The loss of so many people made the Second World War even more tragic.

World War II officially began on September 1, 1939. On that day, troops from Nazi Germany invaded Poland. However, the war did not simply erupt without warning. For years, many dire problems were pushing the world toward war. Some of the worst problems were in Germany.

With America's entry into the war on December 8, 1941, millions of men were called to serve in the nation's armed forces. Millions of other Americans—both men and women—found employment in factories and businesses that supported the war effort.

Man the GUNS Join the NAVY

After World War II, European countries like Great Britain and France could no longer afford to maintain enormous colonial empires. India, an important part of the British Empire, became independent in 1947. Pictured are (left to right) Indian statesmen Jawaharlal Nehru (1869–1964) and Mohandas Gandhi (1869–1948) at a 1946 meeting in Bombay.

During the 1930s, a dangerous man named Adolf Hitler rose to power. Hitler built his Nazi Party using fear and hate. He then went on to take total control of Germany. The German people became fully devoted to him.

Like many other nations in the 1930s, Germany had suffered from the Great Depression. It was an economic crisis that left many people without jobs. In America, President Franklin D. Roosevelt put people back to work. They built schools, libraries, and bridges. In Germany, Adolf Hitler also put people back to work. He had them build tanks, airplanes, and submarines. The German military became very strong. Soon, Hitler was using it to threaten nearby nations.

A similar problem was developing in Japan. In that country, the military was in charge. It demanded absolute loyalty from the Japanese people.

They worked to build weapons of war. Before long, Japan was also threatening its neighbors. In 1937, it launched a full-scale invasion of China. Japanese troops also seized other land in Asia and the Pacific Ocean. These acts created fierce tension between Japan and the United States.

By the end of 1941, every major nation in the world was at war. Germany, Japan, and Italy banded together to form the Axis powers. Those who opposed them were known as the Allies. Many nations joined the Allies, but the three leaders were Great Britain, the Soviet Union, and the United States. Before the war ended in 1945, more than sixty countries took part.

World War II changed America in many ways. With millions of men overseas, women made up a larger part of the workforce. About 3 million women took factory jobs. They showed that they could do the same work as men. African Americans also stepped forward. They fought bravely for their country, even though their country treated them as second-class citizens. When the war was over, many women and African Americans were unwilling to return to a lesser position in American society. World War II caused many other important changes. It affected American business, sports, and the arts.

In 1948, one of the first major crises of the Cold War began when the Soviet Union tried to take control of Berlin. The Soviets blocked roads so that supplies could not get through to parts of the German city controlled by the United States, Great Britain, and France. For nearly a year, supplies had to be flown into Berlin. Finally, the Soviets opened the roads, ending the crisis.

German leader Adolf Hitler (center) was photographed on a balcony in front of the Seine River and Eiffel Tower during a celebratory visit to Paris, June 23, 1940. The German army captured the French capital on June 14, and France surrendered on June 22.

German and Italian Forces on the Move

Europe had been at war since the fall of 1939. However, there were hardly any battles during the first six months. American newspapers called it the Phony War. The quiet was suddenly shattered in the spring of 1940. Heavy fighting proved that this war was for real. Germany and Italy were on the move.

German soldiers gather around a tank commander on a road in the Netherlands, May 1940. German commanders sent tank units ahead of the main army, so they could break through the Allied defenses and cause confusion. The Allies were not able to stop the fast-moving Germany army.

In May 1940, Germany launched a sweeping assault against its western neighbors. German tanks and troops rushed from the Ardennes Forest, which covers parts of Belgium, Luxembourg, and France. The attack caught Germany's enemies by surprise. They had not expected an assault from the Ardennes, believing that it would be too difficult to move an army through the thick woods. Within three weeks, Belgium, Luxembourg, and the Netherlands had all fallen.

The swift German attack continued. It came to be called the blitzkrieg. (*Blitzkrieg*—pronounced BLITZ-kreeg—means "lightning war" in German.) French and British soldiers were unable to stop the blitzkrieg. They kept retreating. Soon nearly four hundred thousand French and British troops could retreat no more. They had been pushed all the way to the sea.

Trucks and other equipment were left on the beach at Dunkirk after the British evacuation in June 1940. The British managed to rescue more than 338,000 men trapped at the harbor. However, they had to leave most of their equipment behind. This meant the British government would have to ask the United States for military supplies.

Firefighters hose down burning buildings in London after a German air raid. In September 1940, the German *Luftwaffe*, or air force, began bombing London and other cities. The attacks on civilian targets became known as the Blitz. Tens of thousands of British civilians were killed and many homes and buildings were destroyed.

The defeated soldiers gathered at a small French harbor town called Dunkirk. The English Channel was behind them. They needed to escape across the waterway, which separates France and Great Britain and is about twenty miles wide at its narrowest point. Otherwise, the soldiers would be killed or captured. British boats frantically sailed across the Channel. Despite attacks by German warplanes, the boats picked up the soldiers and carried them to safety. It was one of the most amazing rescues in history.

After Dunkirk, Hitler's blitzkrieg continued. His army raced on to Paris, the French capital. France was forced to surrender.

Britain stood alone against Germany in Western Europe. Hitler wanted to invade Britain, but the British air force stood in his way. If German troop ships tried to cross the English Channel, British planes would destroy them. From July through October 1940, Hitler's air force tried to defeat the British air force. This huge fight in the sky was called the Battle of Britain. Germany had more planes, but the British pilots were victorious. Hitler was forced to delay his invasion of Britain.

Italian dictator Benito Mussolini was Hitler's ally. Mussolini was also having trouble with his plans for conquest. He tried to capture Greece but failed. Italian troops also struggled against British forces in North Africa. Hitler sent German troops and tanks to help his friend. Hitler also staged his own invasion of Greece. Then he attacked Yugoslavia. The war was rapidly spreading.

America Supports the Allies

In the first years of World War II, the United States did not want to fight in another world war. America was officially neutral, meaning it would not choose sides. However, President Franklin D. Roosevelt hoped the Allies would win. He despised the warlike nature of Hitler and the Axis powers. Quietly, Roosevelt worked to help Great Britain.

In September 1940, the U.S. gave the British navy fifty outdated, but still usable, destroyers. These ships could be used to escort convoys and hunt for submarines. In exchange, the British allowed the United States to establish military bases on Jamaica, the Bahamas, and other Caribbean islands that were part of the British Empire.

The Lend-Lease Act, signed into law March 11, 1941, enabled Allied countries to receive U.S. military aid. Here, young British women examine water-cooled machine guns sent from the United States.

President Roosevelt aided the British by sending them weapons and supplies. In March 1941, Congress passed the Lend-Lease Act. It allowed the president to lend or lease U.S. property to other nations. Roosevelt sent everything from combat boots to cargo ships to old World War I warships. Most of the aid went to Britain and China. Later, the Soviet Union and thirty-four other countries received U.S. help as well.

The Lend-Lease program lasted until the end of the war. America sent roughly $50 billion in equipment to other countries. Lend-Lease was an important part of the Allied war effort. It helped stop the Axis advance.

A section of a twin-engine bomber, provided through the Lend-Lease program, is shown being hoisted aboard ship in an American port.

TROUBLE IN THE EAST

As the fighting raged in Europe, more trouble brewed in Asia and the Pacific. Since 1937, Japan had been at war with China. It was part of Japan's plan to build an overseas empire. By 1941, Japanese commanders had turned their attention toward Southeast Asia. President Franklin D. Roosevelt grew concerned. The Japanese were becoming very powerful. They could threaten the entire region. American territory in the Pacific might even be in danger.

Japan and the United States were close trading partners. The Japanese military relied on American steel and oil. It built ships and planes with

A Chinese Army unit marches in formation, March 1940. China and Japan had been fighting since the early 1930s, although a full-scale war did not begin until 1937. The United States, Britain, France, and the Soviet Union provided financial support to China during the war against Japan.

U.S. steel, and fueled them with U.S. oil. President Roosevelt warned Japan against further aggression. He threatened to halt the sale of steel and oil. Japan ignored his warnings.

In July 1941, Japanese troops pushed deep into Southeast Asia. An angry Roosevelt responded by stopping American exports to Japan. Diplomats from both countries met to discuss the crisis. As the diplomats talked, Japan's leaders planned an attack on the United States. The two nations were drifting toward war.

Communist leader Mao Zedong (left) speaks with Chinese peasants, circa 1940. Mao (1893–1976) led his followers in fighting against the Japanese army until 1945. Afterward, Mao's Communist Party gained control of China. Mao became the first leader of the People's Republic of China in 1949.

This Soviet propaganda poster shows Russian troops repelling the German army. The Cyrillic text reads, "Every Piece of Our Land Is Important." Russians refer to the brutal fighting that followed Germany's surprise 1941 invasion as the Great Patriotic War.

КАЖДЫЙ РУБЕЖ — РЕШАЮЩИЙ!

Germany Invades the Soviet Union

In 1941, Adolf Hitler looked for his next conquest. Two years earlier, he and Soviet dictator Joseph Stalin had made a pledge. They promised not to attack one another. Hitler was known for breaking his promises. He did it once again. Hitler's troops invaded the Soviet Union. It was the biggest invasion in history.

Panzer units of the German Army pass through a blazing Russian village, torched by the evacuees, July 1941. The German tanks are headed toward Moscow.

Soviet troops push an anti-tank cannon through a snowy field near Moscow, late 1941.

There were warning signs of the German attack. Joseph Stalin's spies told him that Hitler was planning an assault. Stalin refused to believe them. He felt certain that Hitler would honor the peace pact. Stalin's trust was shattered on June 22, 1941. On that day, more than 3 million German troops marched into Soviet territory. At first, Stalin's soldiers could not stop the massive blitzkrieg. Adolf Hitler boasted that Germany's invasion of the Soviet Union would be complete in ten weeks.

Joseph Stalin had to slow the German blitzkrieg. He knew that Hitler's soldiers would struggle in the bitter Russian winter. He needed to prevent a German victory before the cold weather arrived. However, winter was still several months away. Stalin decided to trade troops for time. He told his soldiers that they could not retreat. He ordered them to fight to the death. Millions of Soviet soldiers were killed or captured. By November 1941, German tanks were closing in on Moscow, the Soviet capital city. It appeared that Hitler would soon be victorious.

At last, the cold weather struck. Heavy snow and ice quickly covered the battlefield. Weapons and vehicles froze solid. The German soldiers had only their summer uniforms to wear. They struggled just to survive. Joseph Stalin's enormous gamble had paid off. He had sacrificed millions of men to slow the German advance. Now the harsh winter was his ally. Stalin's remaining troops were warmly dressed and ready to fight. It was time for the Soviets to go on the attack.

Adolf Hitler's generals urged him to bring the German soldiers home. The invasion had failed, they said. Hitler refused. He still believed that his troops could beat the Soviets. Germany and the Soviet Union would grapple for the rest of World War II. Their vast conflict included some of the largest battles in history.

This painting shows Russian soldiers preparing to cross a river near Stalingrad, 1942. The Battle of Stalingrad was the bloodiest battle in human history. It lasted for 199 days, and more than a million soldiers and civilians were killed.

...we here highly resolve that these dead shall not have died in vain...

The surprise Japanese attack on the U.S. fleet at Pearl Harbor shocked and angered Americans. The United States immediately declared war against Japan.

REMEMBER DEC. 7th!

Day of Infamy

By the fall of 1941, much of the world was at war. But the United States remained neutral. Many Americans still hoped to avoid the fighting. However, a surprise attack on U.S. soldiers and sailors would quickly change their minds.

In the spring of 1941, Japanese military leaders made the decision to conquer Southeast Asia. The region included British, Dutch, and French colonies. The Japanese hoped that the United States would not become

Fire rages on the deck of USS *Nevada* after the attack on Pearl Harbor. *Nevada* was one of the few American battleships able to maneuver during the attack. However, it was still badly damaged in the raid.

involved in the fighting. But President Roosevelt's strong response to Japan's initial attacks in Southeast Asia worried Japanese leaders. They feared that America might stand in the way of their plans.

The U.S. Navy had a large fleet of ships at Pearl Harbor, Hawaii. Japanese war planners believed that without these ships, America would be helpless to stop Japan from expanding its empire. Throughout the late summer and fall of 1941, Japanese and American diplomats talked about ways to avoid war. At the same time, Japanese military leaders were making plans for a possible attack on Pearl Harbor.

By late November, the decision to attack had been made. A fleet of warships secretly set sail from Japan. There were cruisers, destroyers, battleships, and submarines. Most important, there were six aircraft carriers. The carriers held roughly four hundred airplanes. Even as the Japanese fleet steamed toward Hawaii for a surprise attack, Japanese diplomats continued peace talks in Washington, D.C.

On December 6, American code-breaking specialists intercepted and decoded a long message to the Japanese diplomats. The message convinced President Roosevelt and his aides that Japan was planning to attack very soon.

A burned American B-17 bomber rests near a hangar at Hickam Field. While some of the attacking Japanese planes concentrated on the American fleet, other bombers focused on Pearl Harbor's airfields. More than 85 percent of the American aircraft at Pearl Harbor were destroyed or badly damaged. Most of the planes never even got off the ground.

The USS Arizona Memorial at Pearl Harbor marks the site where this battleship sank during the Pearl Harbor attack. More than a thousand American sailors died on the ship.

But it was impossible to say exactly where. Another intercepted message, decoded on the morning of December 7, indicated that the attack would come that very day, at 1 P.M. Washington, D.C., time. A warning was sent to commanders at Pearl Harbor, but it did not arrive in time.

By 6 A.M. Honolulu time, the Japanese fleet was close enough to Hawaii to start the attack. The first wave of airplanes took off from their carriers. They appeared over Pearl Harbor shortly before 8 A.M.

The American soldiers and sailors were caught completely by surprise. Bullets, bombs, and torpedoes rained down from the sky. A Japanese bomber scored a direct hit on the USS *Arizona*. The huge battleship exploded and sank, killing most of the crew. A second wave of Japanese planes arrived. They swarmed over the harbor and nearby airfields. Seven more battleships were either sunk or damaged. So were thirteen other ships. In addition, more than three hundred U.S. airplanes were destroyed or badly damaged before they could even take off. The ninety-minute attack killed nearly twenty-four hundred soldiers, sailors, and civilians.

But the attack could have been much worse. The U.S. Pacific Fleet's most powerful ships—its three aircraft carriers—were at sea on December 7. Thus, they escaped harm.

Americans were outraged by the sneak attack. The following day, President Roosevelt asked Congress for a declaration of war against Japan. He described December 7, 1941, as "a date which will live in infamy." America joined Great Britain, the Soviet Union, and the other countries known as the Allies. In response, Germany and Italy declared war on the United States.

Japan Seizes British and U.S. Territory

The bombing of Pearl Harbor was just the first step in Japan's plan. Even as the broken ships still burned, other attacks were under way. Japanese troops seized the British colonies of Hong Kong, Burma, Malaya, and Singapore. They also invaded U.S. territory in the Pacific. This included Guam, Wake Island, and the Philippine Islands.

The Philippines invasion began just ten hours after the Pearl Harbor attack. American general Douglas MacArthur was in charge of defending the Philippines. His troops were greatly outnumbered. They tried to hold out at bases in Corregidor and Bataan. Eventually, they were forced to surrender. General MacArthur was ordered to

Japanese troops celebrate the capture of the Bataan Peninsula on the Philippine Islands, April 1942. With a string of rapid conquests in early 1942, the Japanese military seemed unstoppable.

General Arthur Percival, the commander at Singapore, carries a British flag as he prepares to surrender the British stronghold to the Japanese, February 1942. The fall of Singapore, the most important British base in Asia, was a huge blow to the Allies. More than one hundred and thirty thousand British, Indian, and Australian soldiers became prisoners of the Japanese.

leave the Philippines. He vowed someday to return. Meanwhile, the surviving American and Filipino soldiers became prisoners of war. Japanese guards forced them on a brutal, nine-day march. Thousands of prisoners died during the perilous trek. It was called the Bataan Death March.

Japanese leaders misjudged America's response to the early defeats. They thought that the American people would be discouraged and want peace. Instead, the tales of death at Pearl Harbor and Bataan angered most citizens. Americans grew ever more determined to win the war.

This Japanese picture shows American prisoners using improvised litters to carry their comrades who cannot walk. After the fall of Bataan, the Japanese Army forced seventy-five thousand American and Filipino prisoners of war to march about sixty miles to inland prison camps. The prisoners were given little or no food and water. Thousands died during the Bataan Death March.

GERMAN SUBMARINES TERRORIZE THE EAST COAST

Submarines prowl beneath the ocean looking for targets. They can strike a ship without warning. German submarines were known as "undersea boats," or U-boats. In the early months of 1942, U-boats stalked ships off America's East Coast. Submarine attacks were reported from Maine to the Carolinas.

By mid-February, more than fifty cargo ships had been lost. The U-boats were most successful in North Carolina's waters, where Cape Hatteras provided an easy landmark for navigation. American sailors nicknamed the

An Allied tanker sinks after being torpedoed by a German submarine, 1942. Between January and August of 1942, German submarines sank more than six hundred Allied ships.

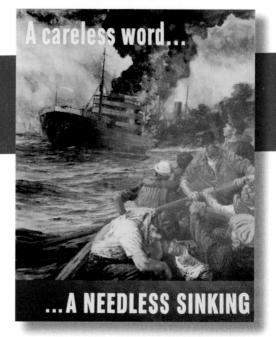

Posters like this one reminded Americans that careless talk about ship departures could be harmful to the war effort. Spies could communicate the news to German U-boats, making the slow-moving Allied ships easy targets.

A careless word...

...A NEEDLESS SINKING

region Torpedo Junction. At night, people on shore heard massive explosions. They saw bright orange fireballs out at sea. The next morning, debris and bodies washed ashore. The submarines were soon attacking ships in the Gulf of Mexico. They also sailed into the mouth of the Mississippi River. By June 1942, about five thousand sailors were dead and nearly five hundred ships had been sunk.

Gradually, the U.S. Navy and Coast Guard learned to deal with the U-boat threat. Ships sailed together in convoys instead of alone. Airplanes patrolled overhead. Pilots searched the water for the sleek, dark outline of a submarine. When a U-boat was spotted, armed aircraft and ships rushed in to attack it. Before long, German submarine captains learned to avoid America's coastline.

Because of the threat of German submarines, U.S. ships began to travel in large groups, called convoys. The convoys were often accompanied by navy destroyers—fast ships that could find and sink subs. Small airplanes or blimps, such as the one pictured above this 1943 convoy, were also used to watch out for threats.

Striking Back in the Pacific

On April 18, 1942, America went on the attack against Japan. A squadron of bombers took off from an aircraft carrier in the Pacific. Lieutenant Colonel Jimmy Doolittle led the planes. They flew at wave-top level toward the islands of Japan. The sixteen planes attacked the capital city of Tokyo and elsewhere. Their bombs caused only minor damage. Yet news of Doolittle's raid thrilled Americans. It also shocked Japan's citizens. They realized that their home islands were not safe from attack.

One of sixteen B-25 bombers takes off from the deck of the USS *Hornet*, on its way to take part in first U.S. air raid on Japan. The Doolittle raid only caused minimal damage to Japanese factories in Tokyo. However, it forced the Japanese to station squadrons of fighter planes in Japan to defend against future attacks. News of the successful raid also boosted American confidence.

Lieutenant Colonel James H. "Jimmy" Doolittle (1896–1993) was a highly decorated American pilot. He earned the Medal of Honor for planning and leading the secret raid on Tokyo in April 1942.

Less than three weeks later, forces of the two nations clashed at sea. It was the Battle of the Coral Sea. Airplanes once again played a key role. Bombers from each side tried to sink enemy ships. American pilots sank more ships than the Japanese pilots sank, but many military historians consider the battle a draw. Coral Sea was the first naval battle in history where the opposing ships never saw each other.

The Battle of Midway took place in June 1942. This time American pilots scored a huge victory. They destroyed three aircraft carriers in five minutes, and sank a fourth Japanese carrier later. The Americans lost one carrier in the battle. It was a crushing blow to the Japanese navy. Slowly, the United States was gaining control of the war in the Pacific.

Navy fighters during the attack on the Japanese fleet off Midway, June 1942. The smoke trail in the lower center of this photo is from a burning Japanese ship.

PLIGHT OF JAPANESE AMERICANS

After the attack on Pearl Harbor, concerns grew about Japanese spies. Many people of Japanese descent lived on the West Coast. The U.S. government feared that some might try to help Japan win the war. In 1942, more than one hundred and twenty thousand Japanese Americans were taken into custody. It was a move that the nation would later regret.

The government built ten camps to hold Japanese Americans during the war. People chosen for the camps came from California, Oregon, Washington State, and Arizona. Families were forced to sell their homes. The camps they

Persons of Japanese ancestry are lined up upon their arrival at the Santa Anita Assembly Center in California, April 1942. From this point, the Japanese Americans were sent to one of ten relocation camps.

These Japanese-American girls were photographed at the Tule Lake Relocation Center in Newell, California. Tule Lake was the largest of the ten relocation centers. It housed more than eighteen thousand Japanese-Americans, and was not closed until 1946.

moved into were crowded and uncomfortable. Two-thirds of camp residents were U.S. citizens. Most were loyal to America. They were being held strictly because of their race.

Despite the unfair treatment, many Japanese-American men volunteered to fight in World War II. The U.S. Army created a special unit for them. It was the 442nd Regimental Combat Team. Its members earned more than eighteen thousand medals for valor during the war. Four decades later, the government admitted its mistake. President Ronald Reagan apologized for the treatment of Japanese Americans during World War II.

Members of the 442nd Regimental Combat Team salute their country's flag during a review at Camp Shelby, Mississippi. This unit was composed primarily of Japanese Americans. The 442nd was sent to fight in Europe, where it participated in battles in Italy, southern France, and Germany between 1943 and 1945.

Women Keep the War Machine Running

The war made demands on nearly every American. Young men were drafted into the armed services. They left their jobs and went overseas to fight. Yet the work they left behind could not stop. Somebody had to build the ships, planes, and tanks needed to win the war. American women took on the task.

Before the war, about 12 million American women were working outside the home. They made up around one-quarter of the U.S. workforce. Most of the jobs women held were in lower-paying fields. Women were maids, secretaries, teachers, nurses, and the like. These jobs were considered suitable for women. Factory jobs were considered men's work. World War II quickly changed that view. With millions of men serving in the military, factories started to hire female workers. Women filled a wide variety of jobs. Some women welded airplane parts together.

Women work on the electronic system of a cargo plane at the Douglas Aircraft Company in Long Beach, California. Without the contributions of female workers at home, the Allies could not have won the war. Women produced the goods that the men used to fight.

Some operated cranes in shipyards. For most, it was their first experience with factory employment. They learned their jobs well and worked long hours.

Rosie the Riveter portrayed the typical working woman. Rosie was an imaginary person. She appeared on posters and billboards encouraging women to take jobs. Rosie the Riveter was patriotic, strong, and determined. By 1945, about 18 million American women were working outside the home. They made up over one-third of the nation's workforce. Another three hundred and fifty thousand women served in the military.

But after the war ended, millions of male veterans returned to the workforce. They again took the higher-paying work. Almost all the women who had been working in the factories lost their jobs.

An African-American woman installs rivets on the fuselage of a bomber at the Consolidated Aircraft Corporation factory in Fort Worth, Texas. The term "Rosie the Riveter" became popular after the illustrator Norman Rockwell depicted a woman named Rosie wearing work clothes and holding a rivet gun on the cover of the *Saturday Evening Post* in May 1943.

ENTERTAINING THE TROOPS

Soldiers fighting a war need many things. They need weapons, food, and clothing. They also need a place to relax when they get a break from the front lines. In 1941, a new group was created to entertain resting soldiers. It was called the United Service Organizations, or USO.

Singer Bing Crosby performs for Allied troops at a USO club in London, August 1944. The clubs were meant to provide a "home away from home" for the soldiers. They often hosted dances, concerts, comedy shows, and other social events for the GIs.

A USO performer entertains a crowd of American soldiers on a troop transport, June 1944.

The USO opened clubs around the world for American soldiers. Each club tried to make the soldiers feel as if they were at home. There were dances, movies, and games. The USO also hosted live shows by Hollywood stars. Famous performers such as Humphrey Bogart, Bette Davis, and Frank Sinatra entertained the troops. By 1944, the USO was hosting seven hundred shows per day around the globe.

American soldiers dance with their dates at a USO club, 1942.

BOB HOPE: HONORARY SOLDIER

Bob Hope was a famous comedian. He was born in England but grew up in the United States. Hope spent much of his career entertaining American soldiers. For fifty years, troops from four different wars laughed at his jokes. For his dedication President Bill Clinton named Hope an honorary veteran in 1997. Bob Hope died six years later at the age of one hundred.

LIFE AT HOME

World War II demanded all of the energy and resources that America could muster. In peacetime, people could buy anything they wished. Wartime was different. Scarce items like food and fuel had to be saved for the troops. The people at home made many sacrifices for the war effort.

The government limited the amount of goods people could buy. For example, there was a shortage of gasoline during the war. The military needed it for jeeps, tanks, planes, and ships. As a result, there was little gas left over for civilians to put in their cars. The government gave out ration coupons. These coupons enabled each family to buy a small amount of gas each week. Rationing ensured that everyone received a fair share. In addition to gasoline, many other scarce items were rationed. These included meat, sugar, butter, and shoes.

During the war, American Boy Scouts distributed posters for the government's Office of War Information. The posters told people how they could support the troops. Scouts also worked as messengers for the Office of Civilian Defense, ran scrap drives, and collected books, socks, and other useful items that could be mailed to American GIs.

Posters like this reminded Americans about the things they could do to help the war effort. These included growing "victory gardens" and participating in salvage programs to recover useful materials, such as steel and rubber, from trash dumps.

Many families began growing their own fruits and vegetables. They planted "victory gardens" in their backyards. By growing their own food, people were helping the war effort. More farm-grown crops were available for the troops. Americans took pride in the sacrifices they made for the war.

Children in Connecticut stage a patriotic demonstration during a Memorial Day parade, 1944.

ISLAND HOPPING IN THE PACIFIC

By 1944, U.S. forces were winning the war against Japan. At the start of the conflict, the Japanese army occupied many islands across the Pacific. American commanders decided to attack only the most important of these islands. They would bypass the rest, leaving isolated Japanese defenders behind as American forces moved ever closer to Japan's home islands. This would help keep the number of American troops killed and wounded as low as possible. The commanders called their plan "island hopping." It worked very well.

The troops who fought in the Pacific sailed on big ships. When it was time to attack an island, they climbed down into smaller boats. These landing craft took them to the beach. As they splashed ashore, the U.S. soldiers began fighting. The Japanese troops fought back. It was usually brutal combat.

General Douglas MacArthur wades ashore during the American landing on the Philippine Island of Leyte, October 1944. The American recapture of the Philippines fulfilled MacArthur's promise after leaving the islands in 1942: "I shall return."

The B-29 bomber, nicknamed "Superfortress," was developed for the war against Japan. The Superfortress had the longest range of any American bomber, about three thousand miles. As American forces gained control of Pacific Islands in 1944, they built airfields. These made it possible for squadrons of B-29s to bomb Tokyo and other important Japanese cities in late 1944 and 1945.

In February 1945, at an island called Iwo Jima, over 6,800 Americans died. Japanese deaths totaled more than 20,000.

Meanwhile, U.S. submarines roamed the Pacific. They sank many Japanese supply ships. The Japanese troops began running out of food and bullets. They strained to defend their islands.

With each new victory, the Americans drew closer to Japan. In November 1944, U.S. bombers began attacking Japan's home islands. Japanese leaders knew that the war was lost. Yet they refused to surrender. The fighting in the Pacific continued.

A member of the 1st Marine Division aims at a Japanese sniper while his companion ducks for cover during the battle for Okinawa. It took three months of fierce fighting (March–May 1945) for American forces to capture the island. Because Okinawa is less than three hundred and fifty miles from the Japanese mainland, American leaders felt the island would make a good base for an invasion of Japan.

A tank carrying a French flag pauses near the Arc de Triomphe, August 26, 1944. The previous day, Allied armies had liberated Paris from German control.

THE ALLIES LIBERATE EUROPE

At first, Adolf Hitler's war machine seemed unstoppable. Then he reached too far. Hitler invaded the enormous Soviet Union. As a result, Germany would have to fight on two huge fronts at the same time. Soviet troops attacked from the east. Meanwhile, the other Allies closed in from the west.

America's entry into the war in 1941 was a fatal blow to Germany. For two years, U.S. troops poured into Britain. They prepared to sail across the English Channel and land in Nazi-held France. The Germans realized an Allied invasion would be coming. They built strong forts along the French coastline to stop it. By the spring of 1944, both sides were ready for a gigantic battle.

American General Dwight D. Eisenhower (1890–1969) was the supreme commander in Europe. Between 1943 and 1945, Eisenhower and his staff planned the Allies' strategies for recapturing Europe from German control. Eisenhower would later be elected the thirty-fourth president of the United States, serving from 1953 to 1961.

The Allied invasion began on June 6, 1944. It was known as D-Day. Most of the attackers were American and British. However, there were also troops from Canada, France, and Poland. The Allies stormed onto beaches in the

French province of Normandy. At some places, the fighting was extremely fierce. German bullets raked the beaches. The bodies of dead soldiers rolled in the surf. However, the Allies forged ahead. By nightfall, they controlled the shoreline.

In the months that followed, American and British forces pushed inland. Vicious battles raged in the French countryside. Gradually, the German troops yielded ground. They fell back toward Germany. The French capital of Paris was liberated in August 1944. Meanwhile, in the east, German soldiers retreated from heavy Soviet assaults. Adolf Hitler's plans for conquest had been reversed. Now Germany struggled just to defend its own borders.

As the Allies freed territory from Nazi rule, they discovered Hitler's concentration camps. The Nazis built these prisons for people they hated,

Under heavy machine gun fire, American soldiers leave the ramp of a landing craft and wade toward the beach at Normandy, June 6, 1944.

The 1940s Decade in Photos: A World at War

These starved Jewish prisoners were freed when American troops arrived at their concentration camp in Austria, May 1945. People in the United States were horrified when they learned about Hitler's plan to eliminate the Jews of Europe. More than five million Jews were killed in territories controlled by the Nazis during World War II.

especially Jewish people. The Allied soldiers who found the camps were horrified. Millions of innocent people had been tortured and killed in these places. Those who survived were starving and ill. The cruelty and suffering of the concentration camps shocked the world.

In December 1944, Hitler's forces made a final assault. They attacked American soldiers in Belgium and Luxembourg. The German advance captured a large area of land. On a map, it looked like a big bulge. As a result, the attack came to be known as the Battle of the Bulge. However, the American troops rallied. They won the ground back. The Battle of the Bulge had been Hitler's last hope. Germany would soon lose the war.

PRESIDENT ROOSEVELT DIES

Franklin D. Roosevelt guided America through some of its toughest times. First, he battled the Great Depression. Later, he inspired hope during the darkest hours of World War II. Roosevelt was a determined man, but by 1944 his health was failing. He passed away in April 1945. A stunned nation mourned.

Even before he became president, FDR had health problems. In 1921, he contracted a serious illness called polio. It robbed him of the use of his legs. Roosevelt refused to accept that he would never walk again. He never let the public see him in a wheelchair. When giving speeches in front of people, he usually stood upright with help from an aide.

President Franklin D. Roosevelt (1882–1945) at his desk in November 1944. That month, he easily won a fourth term as president, earning 432 electoral votes to 99 for the Republican candidate, Thomas Dewey. No one else has ever served more than two terms as president.

In February 1945, President Roosevelt (seated, center) met with Joseph Stalin (seated, right) of the Soviet Union and Winston Churchill (seated, left) of Great Britain. At the Yalta conference, the Allied leaders agreed to a plan for Europe's future at the end of the war. In this photo, Roosevelt's face shows the strain of twelve years as president.

By 1945, Roosevelt was sixty-three years old. The stress of leading a nation during wartime wore on him. He made few public appearances. Those who knew the president were startled by how frail and tired he looked. In April 1945, Roosevelt was resting at a resort in Georgia. On the afternoon of April 12, he complained of a terrible headache. He died quietly a short time later. FDR had poured all of his strength into being president. Yet he did not live long enough to see the Allies' final victory in World War II.

Americans were shocked and saddened by the president's death. For many younger Americans, Roosevelt was the only president they could remember. In this photo, a crowd watches somberly as the president's funeral procession passes through Washington, D.C.

The first atomic bomb explosion, on August 6, 1945, destroyed most of the Japanese city of Hiroshima. About seventy thousand people—mostly civilians—died immediately from the blast. Another thirty thousand Japanese died within a few months from radiation poisoning.

VICTORY IN EUROPE AND THE PACIFIC

In May 1945, Nazi Germany collapsed. Rather than face capture, Adolf Hitler took his own life. The war in Europe was finally over. Around the world, people celebrated. Americans were joyous too. However, they knew there was still much fighting to be done. Japan had yet to surrender.

The Japanese home islands were the last obstacle to victory. Invading these islands would be extremely difficult. The Japanese people would defend them with utter devotion. Many were willing to give their own lives in this defense. Kamikaze pilots were a perfect example. (*Kamikaze* means "divine wind" in Japanese.) These pilots purposely crashed their planes into American warships. More than 2,500 Japanese pilots went on kamikaze suicide missions. They sank dozens of ships. Any invasion by U.S. ground forces would be met with the same zeal. Some American military planners believed that more than half a million

A Japanese pilot makes a *kamikaze* attack, trying to crash his airplane into an American ship, 1945.

A dense "mushroom cloud" of smoke rose more than sixty thousand feet into the air over Nagasaki after an atomic bomb detonated in the Japanese port, August 9, 1945. The next day, Japan's emperor ordered military leaders to surrender to the Allies.

U.S. soldiers might die before Japan surrendered. Estimates of Japanese deaths climbed into the millions.

Harry S. Truman was America's new president. He wanted a better way to achieve victory. Aides told Truman about a secret program called the Manhattan Project. Since 1942, Manhattan Project scientists had been working to build a powerful new weapon called the atomic bomb. The blast from an atomic bomb would be devastating. It could destroy a city. By July 1945, America's first two atomic bombs were ready. President Truman did not hesitate to use them against Japan. He believed that the bombs would cause less loss of life than an invasion would.

A U.S. bomber dropped the first atomic bomb on August 6, 1945. It exploded over the Japanese city of Hiroshima. Roughly seventy thousand people died instantly. Tens of thousands of others were left severely injured, and many of them would die in the coming months. Truman warned that another bomb would be dropped if Japan did not surrender. Japanese leaders refused to do so. Three days after the attack on Hiroshima, another U.S. bomber appeared over the city of Nagasaki. This time forty thousand people were killed instantly.

Japan's leaders at last gave up. On August 14, 1945, they decided to surrender. It was the end of World War II. The Axis powers had been defeated in Europe and the Pacific.

Representatives of the Japanese government arrive aboard the USS *Missouri* in Tokyo Bay to participate in the surrender ceremony, September 2, 1945.

HARRY S. TRUMAN: PLAINSPOKEN PRESIDENT

In 1944, Harry S. Truman—a U.S. senator from Missouri—was elected America's vice president. When Franklin Roosevelt died in April 1945, Truman suddenly became president.

As a young man, Truman had been a farmer. He had volunteered to serve in World War I while in his thirties. Truman was not a gifted speaker, but he was honest and direct. People valued those traits.

Harry S. Truman takes the presidential oath of office, April 12, 1945.

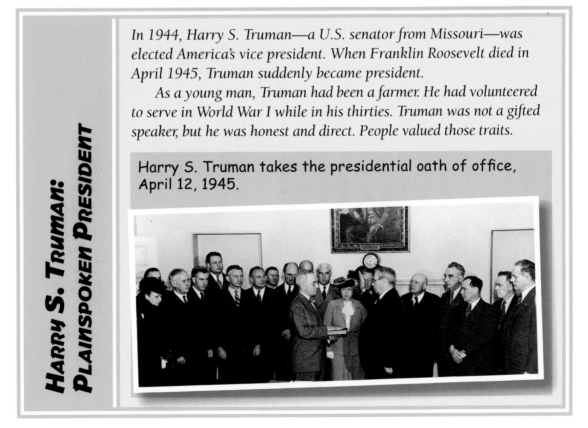

WRITING ABOUT THE WAR

World War II touched nearly everyone's life in some way. Many people wrote about their experiences during the war. One compelling story came from a young girl named Anne Frank. Anne lived in the city of Amsterdam in the Netherlands. Because they were Jewish, Anne and her family had to hide from the Nazis.

This photograph of Anne Frank (1929-1945) was found with her diary after the war ended. It was one of her favorites. "This is a photo as I would wish to look all the time," she wrote. "Then I would maybe have a chance to go to Hollywood."

Dit is een foto, zoals
ik me zou wensen,
altijd zo te zijn.
Dan had ik nog wel
een kans om naar
Holywood te komen.
Annefank.
10 Oct. 1942

The Naked and the Dead, by Norman Mailer (1923–2007), offered a picture of how soldiers in an American platoon worked together.

The Franks hid inside secret rooms in an office building. If found, they would be sent to a concentration camp. For her thirteenth birthday, Anne received a diary. She wrote about her hopes, dreams, and fears. After two years, the Nazis discovered Anne and her family. Most of the Frank family, including Anne, died in a concentration camp. Two years after the war ended, her diary was published. Anne's story gave a face to the tragedy of the Holocaust.

Author Norman Mailer wrote about the typical soldier's experience. His book was titled *The Naked and the Dead*. It described the terror of combat and the boredom of army life. Mailer was a U.S. soldier in the Pacific during the war. He based the novel on his real-life experiences. *The Naked and the Dead* was first published in 1948. Today, it is regarded as one of the best war books ever.

"So true, so dramatic, so heart-warming!"

LOUELLA PARSONS, Cosmopolitan Magazine

Samuel Goldwyn's

"The BEST Years of Our Lives"

starring

Myrna Loy • Fredric March • Dana Andrews
Teresa Wright • Virginia Mayo • Hoagy Carmichael
and introducing Cathy O'Donnell and Harold Russell
Directed by William Wyler • Screen Play by Robert E. Sherwood
From a novel by MacKinlay Kantor • Released thru RKO Radio Pictures

Acclaimed by critics as "The greatest picture to come from Hollywood in a long time"

During the 1940s, Hollywood made many movies about the war and its aftermath. *The Best Years of Our Lives* (1946) was a drama about the family problems that soldiers faced after returning home from World War II.

Breaking Through the Color Barrier

Baseball was America's favorite sport. For decades, however, black players were banned from the major leagues. In 1947, a talented black infielder broke through baseball's color barrier. His name was Jackie Robinson.

Robinson was born in Georgia in 1919. He was a sports star in high school and college. During World War II, he served as an officer in the U.S. Army. Robinson disliked the army's rule about keeping black soldiers and white soldiers separate. This practice was called segregation. In the 1940s, segregation still existed in many parts of American society. After the war, Jackie Robinson chose to confront segregation in major league baseball.

The Brooklyn Dodgers (now the Los Angeles Dodgers) gave Robinson his chance. Their general manager was a white man named Branch Rickey.

Jack Roosevelt "Jackie" Robinson (1919–1972) played ten seasons for the Brooklyn Dodgers. Today, all major league baseball teams have retired his number, 42, as a sign of respect for his important place in the game's history.

Racial discrimination was a part of American life during the 1940s. In Southern towns, whites and African Americans were segregated, with separate schools, entrances to theaters and restaurants, sections of buses, and even drinking fountains. However, attitudes about race would begin to change in the late 1940s and 1950s.

He too believed that segregation was wrong. He hired Jackie Robinson to play for the Dodgers.

Many fans—and even other baseball players—insulted Robinson. They booed and heckled him when he took the field. Robinson ignored them. He focused on playing baseball. He was voted Rookie of the Year in 1947. During his major league career, he batted .311 and played in six All-Star Games. Jackie Robinson's success convinced other teams to sign black players. Baseball's color barrier disappeared. Other types of segregation in America began to disappear also.

Jackie Robinson (right) is pictured with teammates (from left) Johnny "Spider" Jorgensen, Harold "Pee Wee" Reese, and Eddie Stanky on the dugout steps during Robinson's first official game, April 15, 1947.

Gandhi's Legacy of Peace

Mohandas Gandhi was an important Indian leader. He played a major role in helping India obtain independence. Gandhi was a peaceful man. He taught that freedom could be achieved without violence. The Indian people called him Mahatma, which means "great soul."

The British government had gained control of India during the mid-1700s. In 1858, India officially became a British colony. Because India is rich in natural resources, it was

As a young man, Mohandas K. Gandhi (1869–1948) was educated as a lawyer in London. He later worked to help the Indian community in the British colony of South Africa. In 1915, Gandhi returned to India and began fighting for Indian independence.

sometimes called "the highest jewel in the British crown." However, during the early 1900s, some Indians wanted to break away from Britain. They wanted to make India an independent country again.

Gandhi found peaceful ways to protest British rule. For example, he advised Indians not to pay

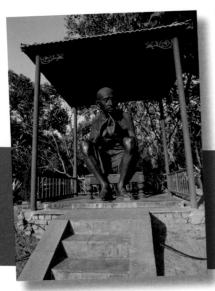

This statue depicts Gandhi in a thoughtful pose. In 1942, Gandhi demanded that the British should withdraw from India. He hoped that because of the war, Britain would give in to Indian pressure and grant the country independence. However, the British authorities responded by arresting Gandhi and other Indian leaders.

At a meeting in June 1947, Lord Louis Mountbatten, Britain's viceroy of India, unveiled a plan to divide British India into two independent countries, India and Pakistan. Pictured are (left to right) Indian leader Jawaharlal Nehru, British advisor Lord Ismay, Mountbatten, and Indian Muslim leader Muhammad Ali Jinnah.

their taxes. He also told Indians not to buy things made in Britain. The British government arrested Gandhi many times. While in jail, he often refused to eat. These fasts worried the British authorities. They knew that the Indian people would revolt if Gandhi starved to death in prison.

In 1947, Gandhi saw his dream come true when India gained its independence. A year later, a religious fanatic shot and killed him. The assassin was an Indian Hindu. He was angry that Gandhi had helped Indian Muslims to create the state of Pakistan.

Gandhi was seventy-eight years old when he died. The world mourned his passing. During the 1950s and beyond, Gandhi's work inspired many other peaceful movements around the globe. In the United States, Martin Luther King adopted Gandhi's methods to draw attention to the problems facing African-Americans.

Gandhi's tomb at Rajghat in New Delhi is lit by an eternal flame.

Gandhi's Legacy of Peace

Looking Ahead

The tragedy and turmoil of the 1940s changed the world in fundamental ways. International power shifted. Old empires collapsed, and new countries emerged. Two Allied countries that had fought together to defeat the Axis powers in World War II now began a long, bitter political struggle with each other.

At the start of the 1940s, European countries had controlled large overseas empires. But World War II had left Europe in ruins. European economies were in shambles. The European empires began to break up. In 1947, after a long campaign for independence led by Mohandas K. Gandhi, Britain gave up India, its most important colony. Two independent countries were created: India and Pakistan. France tried to hold on to its colonies but faced an exhausting war in Vietnam.

The Nazis had murdered millions of Jews during World War II. But survivors of the Holocaust and other Jews established a Jewish country, Israel. The new country was officially declared in May 1948, but Israel had to defeat its Arab neighbors in a war to survive. Though the fighting from that war was over by the beginning of 1949, the Arab-Israeli conflict was never resolved.

In 1949, communist forces won a civil war in mainland China. On October 1, Mao Zedong declared the establishment of the People's Republic of China. A communist country, it was at first an ally of the Soviet Union.

This was not good news for the United States. America and the Soviet Union had become bitter rivals. A conflict known as the Cold War had begun. Although this struggle was very tense, the armed forces of the United States and the Soviet Union did not fight each other directly. Instead, the two superpowers tried to get other countries to support their political and economic systems, and to prevent the other side from gaining allies. In Eastern Europe, the Soviet Union installed communist governments that answered to Soviet leaders. Meanwhile, the United States—under the administration of President Truman—crafted policies to prevent Western European countries from becoming communist. For example, under the Marshall Plan, the United

States spent billions of dollars to rebuild Western Europe. The North Atlantic Treaty Organization (NATO) was an alliance of European countries, the United States, and Canada. It was formed in 1949 to counter the threat of communist expansion.

As the 1950s dawned, people in the United States, the Soviet Union, and all over the world worried about a direct war between the superpowers. With atomic weapons, missiles, and jets—all developed during the 1940s—unimaginable destruction could come quickly and with little warning.

Elvis Presley would be one of the most famous performers of a new musical style during the 1950s: rock and roll.

CHRONOLOGY

1940—German troops attack Belgium, Luxembourg, the Netherlands, and France in May. British and French troops are rescued from Dunkirk in late May and early June. The Battle of Britain rages through October.

1941—Congress approves the Lend-Lease Act in March. Germany invades Russia in June. Japan launches a surprise attack against U.S. forces at Pearl Harbor, Hawaii, on December 7.

1942—German U-boats raid U.S. shipping along the East Coast. In April, U.S. bombers stage the Doolittle Raid against Japan. The Battle of Midway takes place in June. The U.S. government begins detaining Japanese Americans on the West Coast.

1943—U.S. forces in the Pacific capture the island of Guadalcanal in February. Soviet troops begin repelling the German invasion. Allied soldiers liberate North Africa in May.

1944—Allied forces land at Normandy, France, on June 6. U.S. bombers begin attacking the Japanese home islands in November. Adolf Hitler makes a final attempt at victory with the Battle of the Bulge in December.

1945—President Franklin D. Roosevelt dies of natural causes in April. Harry Truman becomes president. Nazi Germany surrenders in May. Japan surrenders in August following the destruction of Hiroshima and Nagasaki by U.S. atomic bombs.

1946—The United Nations holds its first meeting in January. Tensions mount between the United States and the Soviet Union. Their rivalry will grow into a struggle called the Cold War that will last for half a century.

1947—Anne Frank's *The Diary of a Young Girl* is first published. Jackie Robinson breaks the ban on black players in major league baseball.

1948—The Berlin Airlift begins in June. It provides food and medicine to the city of Berlin, Germany, which is under Soviet blockade. Harry Truman remains president after defeating Thomas Dewey in the November election.

1949—The Soviet Union tests its first atomic bomb in August. The communist People's Republic of China is established in October.

GLOSSARY

aggression—An unprovoked invasion or other hostile act.

atomic bomb—A very powerful weapon that releases nuclear energy.

blitzkrieg—Meaning "lightning war" in German, it is a swift attack by troops, tanks, and planes.

bomber—An airplane built to carry and drop bombs.

civilian—A person who is not a member of the armed forces.

concentration camp—A Nazi-run prison where Jews, Gypsies, and other people considered undesirable were tortured and executed.

convoy—A group of ships or other vehicles traveling together for safety.

custody—The condition of being detained or held under guard.

debris—Rubble or wreckage.

diplomat—A government official who carries out negotiations with representatives of other countries.

exports—Goods traded or sold to another country.

Holocaust—The large-scale murder of European Jews and others by the Nazis.

kamikaze—Meaning "divine wind" in Japanese, it refers to pilots who carried out suicide attacks on U.S. ships.

ration—A fixed portion of goods or supplies.

segregation—The practice of keeping people separate based on race or other differences.

torpedo—A self-propelled underwater bomb launched by a submarine, ship, or airplane.

valor—Courage or bravery, especially in battle.

FURTHER READING

Bobek, Milan, editor. *Decades of the Twentieth Century: The 1940s*. Pittsburgh, Pa.: Eldorado Ink, 2005.

Haugen, Brenda. *Joseph Stalin: Dictator of the Soviet Union*. Mankato, Minn.: Compass Point Books, 2006.

Hoyt, Edwin P. *Pearl Harbor Attack*. New York: Sterling Publishing, 2008.

Langley, Andrew. *Hiroshima and Nagasaki: Fire from the Sky*. Mankato, Minn.: Compass Point Books, 2006.

Platt, Richard. *D-Day Landings: The Story of the Allied Invasion*. New York: DK Publishing, 2004.

Provost Beller, Susan. *Battling in the Pacific: Soldiering in World War II*. Minneapolis, Minn.: Twenty-First Century Books, 2008.

Rice, Earle. *Blitzkrieg! Hitler's Lightning War*. Hockessin, Del.: Mitchell Lane Publishers, 2008.

Robinson, Sharon. *Promises To Keep: How Jackie Robinson Changed America*. New York: Scholastic, 2004.

Sakurai, Gail. *Japanese-American Internment Camps*. New York: Children's Press, 2007.

Stein, R. Conrad. *The Home Front During World War II in American History*. Berkeley Heights, N.J.: Enslow Publishers, 2003.

Internet Resources

<http://www.history.com/minisites/worldwartwo>
This site, maintained by the History Channel, provides detailed accounts of battles, a timeline of the D-Day landing, and fascinating video clips.

<http://www.rosietheriveter.org/>
Learn more about the efforts of America's female workers during World War II. This site by the Rosie the Riveter Trust contains a wide variety of information.

<http://www.jackierobinson.com/>
The official site of Jackie Robinson, it contains a complete history of the celebrated baseball player.

INDEX

Nazi Party, 6, 42–43, 50–51, 56
See also Germany
Nehru, Jawaharlal, 6, 55
Netherlands, 9, 10, 50
North Atlantic Treaty Organization (NATO), 57

Okinawa, 39

Pakistan, 55, 56
Pearl Harbor, Hawaii, 20–23
Percival, Arthur, 25
Philippine Islands, 24–25, 38
Poland, 5, 41
Presley, Elvis, 57

rationing, 36–37
Reagan, Ronald, 31
Reese, Harold ("Pee Wee"), 53
relocation camps, 30–31
Rickey, Branch, 52–53
Robinson, Jackie, 52–53
Rockwell, Norman, 33

Roosevelt, Franklin D., 6, 12–13, 14–15, 22, 23
death of, 44–45, 49
"Rosie the Riveter," 33

segregation, 52–53
Singapore, 24, 25
Soviet Union, 7, 13, 14, 23, 56–57
Germany's invasion of the, 16–19, 41
sports, 52–53
Stalin, Joseph, 17–19, 45
Stanky, Eddie, 53
submarines, 26–27, 39

Truman, Harry S., 48, 49, 56

U-boats, 26–27
United Service Organizations (USO), 34–35

"victory gardens," 37

Wake Island, 24
women workers, 32–33
World War II, 4–5, 7, 56
America helps the Allies, 12–13
and the atomic bomb, 46, 48
beginning of, 5, 9–11
and concentration camps, 42–43, 51
end of, 40–43, 46–49
and factories, 5, 7, 32–33
and German submarines, 26–27
Germany invades the Soviet Union, 16–19, 41
and internment of Japanese Americans, 30–31
Pacific battles, 24–25, 28–29, 38–39
Pearl Harbor attack, 20–23
and rationing, 36–37
and troop entertainment, 34–35

Yugoslavia, 11

PICTURE CREDITS